THE DEBT DETOX

THE DEBT DETOX

Cleanse Your Finances, Rebuild Your Life

ELIAS HARTLEY

QuantumQuill Press

CONTENTS

CHAPTER 1

Introduction

The problem isn't that there aren't any solutions out there. As a race, Americans are experts at alternative options. The problem is that we're not aware, not willing, or simply don't believe that real and life-altering lifestyle changes are necessary in order to rectify our financial crises. It's these pervasive, convoluted, skewed views of money that keep us deep in debt and subject to the emotional shackles it brings with it. You can decide to become financially secure. You can decide to lead a life dictated by your own interests and pursuits instead of one imposed upon you by financial obligation. You can decide to walk through this program with the faith that radical changes are not the critical lifestyle upheavals that might be painful or uncomfortable. Rather, they are the transformative, natural extensions of your march toward financial peace.

What is the Debt Detox? The quick and dirty: it's a monthlong comprehensive program created to take folks out of their deep, dark, debt-laden fodders and get them on the path to becoming debt-free. And though I understand that "getting out of debt" is a common pledge that we humans like to write down on various New Year's resolutions, I assure you, the Debt Detox is different. This is not about skimping and saving your way to paying off a credit card or two. This is about making permanent and healthy lifestyle changes that will result in never again being a regular presence in the Land of Brokedom. Does that sound extreme or challenging or unrealistic? If so, I can understand. We live in a materialistic, consumer-driven society. But I'm happy to say that millions of people all over the country are debt-free without having to compromise their quality of life. You should be, too.

CHAPTER 2

Understanding Debt

A bond or debenture is a long-term debt. A bondholder is promised a fixed amount of interest every year, whereas a debenture holder is only paid at the end of the term of the debenture. A loan is money borrowed from a bank or finance company. The amount is repaid according to a repayment schedule, and an interest rate is charged on the principal amount of the loan, which determines the amount repaid. The interest rate associated with loans can be either variable or fixed. Furthermore, loans are divided into short-, medium-, and long-term loans. Finance leases are different from traditional leases, in that the entity leasing the equipment or property accepts the owner's rights and obligations to repairing and maintaining the asset. In addition, the entity leasing makes fixed payments over a set period and might apply for ownership at the end of the lease term. A financial institution like an insurance company, bank, or business organization usually assumes the role of a lessor.

The topic of debt traces back to ancient times with its definition layered in meaning. Debt is what someone owes another person, and as an adjective, it refers to an item that is owed. So, a debt is an amount of money that has been borrowed by a person or an organization, usually based on an agreement. According to Collins English Dictionary, debt is the state or condition of owing something. A debt can also be an action. For example, if someone is in debt to you, they owe you something, especially money. By that definition, a variety of material principles exist, and those who use secondary sources bring a newer perspective to the discourse on debt. As I was researching debt, I discovered that many people oppose it. It is generally not approved of because it cultivates consumer borrowing habits.

CHAPTER 3

Assessing Your Financial Situation

Another important part of this step is determining what kind of life and lifestyle you want to have. This will help you determine how much money you need and how many years you need to keep working or start your own business. Starting your own business will require more risk and investment in the short term, but it will give you more time and money in the long term. While people tend to be driven by their emotions and desires, this is not always the best course of action. That said, you should allow yourself to interpret what you can pay for and how much money you can make to maintain your desired lifestyle.

In addition to listing your assets and liabilities, you will need to average the cost of essential items, such as: - Food - Gasoline - Mortgage, rent or other living expenses - Clothing - Utilities - Other outgoings

Now study your assets and liabilities to determine your net worth. Note: very few people start out in the positive. Also, the numbers may seem shocking, but remember that this point is simply to see where you are starting from so that you can set measurable goals.

Next, list all of your assets, tangible and intangible, such as: - Cash - Pension plans - Stocks - Businesses - Rental properties - Investment properties - Personal property

Now that you understand the big picture, it is time to take a clear look at your financial situation. You can use basic personal financial software to do this, and you can download it for free, but all you truly need is a pen, paper and your bank statements. Here is what you want to do. First, write down all of your outstanding liabilities, such as: - Credit card debt - Personal loans - Overdraft protection - Mortgages - Business loans - Student loans - Car loans - Store cards

CHAPTER 4

Creating a Budget

Periodically, prepare a monthly revenue or investment report, which will help you improve your ability to understand the plan.

Use the income and expenditures part at the bottom to evaluate whether you can finally stay at home, work for an afternoon, or participate in certain parties. When you have finished with the budgetary part of the bile, go over all the supplementary expenses. Use your financial statements to reinforce what you have just done and show how well you understand the link between your income and expenses.

Don't budget additional money for the purchase of luxury items. The only time you should buy luxury is when you pay the singee, have put a heavy amount into savings, and not in a way that sacrifices the hybrids that the convenient rey for the loan should serve.

It isn't difficult to list your monthly bills. Chances are, to pay each one you will need to have some money left over after the bills are paid, so that you can eat, get to work, and purchase essentials at the store. And don't forget to include extra expenditures, like school supplies, visits home, or other occasional costs.

In a budget, you list all of your monthly expenditures in one column and in the next, the amount you will plan to spend according to both your needs and resources. Essential monthly bills, such as power, car loan, rent/mortgage, insurance, and health insurance, should also be included in the budget.

A budget must account for everything you spend money on. This includes monthly bills, debt repayments, daily purchases, and any money you put aside in savings for fun or charitable giving. Life in the debt detox is not about suffering deprivation. It is simply about understanding the choices you have and how those choices will affect you far into the future. Essentially, it's about building a conscious financial plan.

CHAPTER 5

Cutting Expenses

The truth is, there are trade-offs to make and a short-term, embarrassment-free path does not exist. The financial diet initially is not easy – but not for long. With only a modicum of fiscal responsibility, the first financial accomplishment comes quickly: The debt detox should start making you feel better in just thirty days. If the previous section exhaustively detailed the obvious, there are some less dramatic sacrifices you may also be able to make that can serve to save on expenses as well. If you are a homeowner, consider potentially painful scenarios: renting out a room just to get through your current financial quagmire (a debt detox may be similar to entering a nightmare; the sleep overpowered by danger, the escape is always near, closer than any hope). Once the property market rebounds, well, perhaps your lodgers can be convinced to vacate politely.

Be scrupulous about using what you already have. Doing without, even for a short while, can be good for your superego and great for your pocketbook. Before heading out to shop, especially for clothes or other consumer goods, analyze what you've already got. A bit of tailoring or a new hem can do wonders with an existing wardrobe; a bit of polish or a good scrub can make what has been neglected look like new. This is not to say you should become some unbathed avowed minimalist, but chances are you don't really need what you're tempted to buy as much as you believe you do. At least for now. Now is the time for frugal chic. The next essentials are everything. Assuming you are similarly resolved, you may find yourself able to derive personal satisfaction by self-sacrifice (I'm not suggesting anyone derive personal satisfaction from self-deprivation).

CHAPTER 6

Increasing Income

Now, there is no need for anyone to vanish into the woods, but being obliging will help. Realize that you can take some simple and practical steps to avoid the debt perils that others wallow in. You should view page 104 as a statement of guiding financial principles, as strict commandments to be obeyed as far as you can, unless the standard answers do not apply to you. But you must also say, "I'm not a theoretician, I'm just someone getting through life the best way I know. I will maybe manage to stick to four of the top seven commandments, maybe all seven. How about you?" The next page sets out two pages of practical do's and don'ts, followed by questions that the realistic reader is likely to seek answers to. Accept that there isn't any great mystery to finding the way out of debt to a sounder and more peaceful financial future: it's just a matter of rolling up your sleeves and getting on with it. But be careful of the pitfalls, and think.

There was a fable born of the subprime mortgage meltdown in the United States that began a few years back. Part of the problem was that some lenders were lending money to borrowers that had no capacity to pay them back, a situation that led to much misadventure and ruins on both sides of the debt contract. The fable goes something like this: A fox invited a rabbit over for dinner, and being the considerate host, asked the rabbit what he enjoyed eating. The rabbit replied that he liked eating roots, so that was exactly what the fox booked for dinner. Realizing that it was about to become the main ingredient at a banquet, the rabbit panicked, his instincts kicking in. "I'm a rabbit," he reminded himself, "I can run. I will be just fine as long as I stay close to my warren," and he vanished into the woods.

CHAPTER 7

Building an Emergency Fund

Durland suggests engaging the competitive spirit by making it a contest: Make a goal for how much you're earmarking for your emergency fund, and—here's the fun part—mobilize your friends to try to beat you to it. Make it a "race" and cheer each other on as you complete the task of amassing the money. The first one there wins! Once you've grown your account to your target amount, put some of it in a simple one-month time deposit at your community bank. That way, you won't be tempted to raid your fund to treat yourself to something you can't afford if the money's too accessible. But in case of a true emergency, the bank will allow you to tap your funds if you pay the penalty. With this approach, you'll still earn better interest than you would using a standard savings account.

Just when you least expect it, life throws you a financial curveball. Your car needs a new transmission; medical bills arrive in the mailbox; the company you work for goes belly-up and you suddenly find yourself without a paycheck. Having a cash reserve will help provide security and peace of mind in case you suddenly find yourself without a regular stream of income or if you're faced with an expensive, unpredictable emergency. J.R. Durland, owner of SC Financial Services, LLC in Aurora, Colorado, suggests building an emergency fund even as you pay off high-interest credit cards.

CHAPTER 8

Paying Off High-Interest Debt

Developing and following a strict budget will rein in demand for your debt if you devote every available penny to repaying your creditors. Abstain from using the credit card accounts that you are generally trying to repay. Concentrate the extra money on the account with the highest interest rate until you eliminate it as quickly as possible. Then, transfer that monthly payment to the account with the next highest balance and continue the process. If your accounts have similar high interest rates, attack the debt with the largest balance first, since it will save you the most money and time in the long run. Repeat the process until you're out of debt. Remember that you can always postpone saving money for your financial future while you're paying off high-interest debt. After all, exercising a good habit on a daily basis will add to your financial well-being over time.

It's usually a good idea to concentrate first on high-interest debt, such as credit card balances, finance company loans, and payday lending stores. Paying off high-interest debt can yield immediate savings and the relief that comes with ridding yourself of oppressive, costly commitments. You should approach paying off high-interest debt even if you're not able to follow through with the full Debt Detox Plan. Reducing your overall expenses, raising funds to increase your disposable income, shopping around for the lowest-interest rates, and learning how to negotiate with your creditors will leave you in a better position to enhance your financial status and plan your future.

CHAPTER 9

Exploring Debt Consolidation Options

This is the kind of picture that many people have when contacting someone to help them get control of their debt. How can I get this money off my back so I can live and enjoy life again? If the amount involved is small enough, such as below $5,000.00, and you have an excellent credit rating, you might be best able to handle these problems through a series of low-interest transfers. As credit card companies get desperate to generate cash, more and more are offering time-limited loans at five percent or lower, hoping that you won't mind so much when the rate climbs up over 20 percent after twelve months. If you are savvy, you can do the math and transfer these loans over and over, until you have gotten them down to zero. With careful planning and constant vigilance, a person with good credit can figure out how to work the system, paying minimal interest on the back of these loans, until they get them down to zero.

You might owe a great deal of money to credit cards and quickly find that you are paying out an enormous sum of money towards these bills every month. Moreover, with interest rates of 25, 30, or even 35 percent in some cases, hardly a dime of every minimum payment is going towards the actual principle you owe. You may be current with your payments, and barely staying above water, but there are other warning signs of an underlying debt problem: If your credit card bills keep going up, even though you are not using the cards; If you find that the only way you pay off your monthly bills is by taking out another loan, or opening up yet another credit card; If you pay all your bills off each month and then find the credit limits on your card decrease, then your finance charges increase to the point you cannot possibly pay the monthly minimums; or If you find that your opportune spending (buying today, paying off tomorrow) could give you a cash flow crunch within three months, you could be courting real trouble.

In the first stages of the Debt Detox process, I'll introduce you to various types of debt. Now, I want to explore various options for consolidating this debt. Many people are surprised to learn the many options available to them when considering how to handle their various debts. Depending on how much you owe, who you owe, the interest rates you are paying, and more, all sorts of factors come into play when deciding what, if anything, is best as far as a consolidation option, and which consolidation option makes the most sense. Here are a few things to consider.

CHAPTER 10

Negotiating with Creditors

Do you own this debt or are you a collector? Am I liable to pay this debt? How much do I still owe? Should payment be made to you, or is there a way to pay the original debtor? When do you require payment by? Is there any way to reduce the figure I owe you today?

Questions to ask creditors—before hanging up:

If you are in a tough financial position, creditors and bill collectors can be very intimidating. They use fear, shame, and guilt as tactics in order to get you to pay them before you pay yourself. The best way to communicate with creditors is from a position of calm, grace, and maturity. Don't make excuses about why you can't make payment. Do not allow their words to guilt or shame you into paying before it is time. Most people take the bait on this because they do not negotiate with their creditors soon and often enough. If for any reason you are incapable of speaking with your creditors in a calm manner, ask them to call back later or allow another person to handle the call. Another option is to deal with the problem in writing. More often than not, one must not be cautious of threats of taking legal action against you. It is very rare for this to happen. And if it does, punishment measures are usually less severe than what the creditor has threatened.

CHAPTER 11

Developing a Debt Repayment Plan

Step 1: Gather all the pieces of personal data you have for each loan - interest rates, if variable, the highest approach rate, and the range at which the rate has fluctuated and the low point. Step 2: Decide how much in total (or separately by month or quarter) you can afford to pay in order for all of your debts to be paid off in 2-3 years. Step 3: Acquire an awareness of your loan type and then determine whether you should pay off secured or unsecured loans first. Step 4: Use four additional levels of priority as provided by the following factors to give you more direction on how to repay the funds you owe. Step 5: Take your highest priority loan and slightly increase its monthly payment or pay off the loan at the earliest opportunity. Step 6: When that loan is debt-free, take the same approach as in Step 5 with each year. Step 7: By the time you're finished with one of the first four levels, move up to the next level, with monthly payments from debt-free loans being thrown to the next lower priority loan, thus increasing the speed of payment and levels of your priority debts.

You're ready to punch your way out of debt, but here's the problem: you're not sure how to prioritize which debts to tackle first or what specific repayment strategy you should implement. You've already ruled out filing for bankruptcy and won't let debt consolidation or hiring a debt settlement company bleed you dry. So, you figure developing and sticking to a debt repayment plan over the next 24-36 months will be your best option. Taking that route means you have to know when and in what order to pay off your debts. By the time you're about to read the next chapter, you should know the distinction between secured and unsecured loans, and how to deal with each. Here's an overview of the seven-step process I will take you through. At the end of the process, you will know around what time each of your debts should become debt-free, leading to $150k-$500k over 2-3 years.

CHAPTER 12

Tracking Your Progress

On your cash flow statement, list every income source you have and calculate how much comes in weekly or monthly. Also, list all your expenses - the exact amounts of your fixed expenses and estimated sums for your variable necessities and undesirables. Regularly compare your projected expenses with what you actually spend to notice trends and control excesses. For example, you might expect to spend $200 a month on clothing - occasional replacement of the kids' outgrown shoes, or replenishment after you gain - or lose - ten pounds. But if you notice you're spending more, perhaps you're using the mall as a buffer against stress, and you should spend some evenings at the library instead. You might learn something, or you could at least find some books on the causes of compulsive shopping.

To maintain momentum, monitor your progress. You'll need a balance sheet and a cash flow statement - just as you would if you were running a business. And you are - the business of your life. Instead of profits and losses, your balance sheet reflects your net worth - your assets versus your liabilities. Every month, add up the actual totals, compare the changes from one period to the next, and identify trends. Your net worth will increase until you have zero debt, and you can invest your surplus funds.

CHAPTER 13

Avoiding Debt Traps

Now we are getting stung. The only difference is the name they give themselves to wear away your resistance. Payday loan, installment credit, signature line of credit. It really doesn't matter. There are three criteria in determining if you are working with a loan shark. First, now they actually charge rates about 20 percent! So the rate is greater than ten percent. Now it is really about 20 percent that has been pretty well confirmed from all the various studies. They also are willing to take your assets if you can't repay at unheard of terms... your home, your car, your retirement accounts, investments. This tends to push people further and further out of the workforce, or lay their estates barren.

Loan sharks still exist today, but they seem more legitimate. They will take all your assets. A traditional mid-20th century usury rate was 5 percent, and loan sharking is often defined as charging rates of more than 10 percent. So let's turn our gaze from those taking small loans to keep utilities on or to buy groceries. We have gotten so absorbed in low income, but more often predatory lending that we ignored the loan sharks coming into the mid sections of our economy, and then burgeoning in the swelling high income era.

CHAPTER 14

Managing Credit Cards Wisely

Short of cash, tight need to you are, avoiding the truth is not the answer. The truth is, making only the minimum monthly payment over your lifetime could triple your credit-card debt. What results over time can feel like a debt financial detox. Your point bank balance, screaming at your pay stub: wave "Hasta la vista" to the fun day-to-day. Too much of a future paycheck applied before you actually get it off. And those purchases you made become so very, very wrinkly. Little parcels, wrapped in autumn cash, are tossed in the direction of overblown credit-card companies to reduce minimum payments, only to inflate statements all over again. Now the big picture - that $6,000 in holiday gifts you'd actually paid $14,074 for. (That's at the average 17% annual interest rate).

The fact is, most of us don't have time to figure out what's driving up our credit-card balances or even the shame factor associated with choosing debt. So we basically choose the easiest, most convenient route, which is to pay the absolute bear minimum. You rationalize. Besides, what difference does $10 or $50 make if you're paying $10,000 anyway? Big difference.

Just charge it. That little plastic pie is a cinch to swipe. It's fun. And exciting. The truth is that using credit cards can be a lot like waiting for the other shoe to drop, especially if at the end of the month, you're short of cash or the balance from the prior month has just about wiped you out. The other less than pleasant aspect of using credit cards is often the high cost associated with carrying a balance on them. We all know the credit-card drill. You charge on Monday and repay on the day of judgment, otherwise known as the credit-card due date. Give or take a few days. A little more here, a little more there. You can reason with yourself. I'll pay it off. I know I will. But if for any reason I can't, it's only because I had to pay my [rent, mortgage, car note, herculean cable bill].

CHAPTER 15

Saving for the Future

When dealing with personal finances, each financial component is important primarily because of its impact on your present life or in the future. I am constantly talking about how more important the present is than the future but when it comes to managing your personal finances, most of the key components deal with future financial issues. Each key financial component is a little like insurance. We can't predict when we'll need it but when we do, we're glad we have it. They don't prevent the bad from happening but they provide victims of the bad time to recover and heal. Each of these key financial components reduces your stress about life's possible curve balls. When employed, they can even provide peace of mind. As detailed and sometimes boring as this might be, the entire financial industry is built around a foundation of insurance and future security: loans, debt, and potential income.

No one will ever care about your future as much as you do. To some people, this chapter title looks like it has a couple of snooze-worthy topics about retirement, emergency funds, and insurance. Bleh. People don't want to read about that boring stuff. But wait. We've already covered the scary statistics about those who will retire without enough funds to live on, as well as the yikes! nature of life's many curve balls. This is real-world information that you need to hear. The solution? You need to dive into the details of retirement, emergency funds, and insurance and then get on with your life.

CHAPTER 16

Investing for Financial Growth

Social Security was proffered as a solution to old-age poverty. Throughout its history, the program has evolved into a payroll tax-financed political slush fund. Despite such abuses, current workers have been led to believe that politicians can keep promises made decades ago to their retired predecessors. They cannot. The number of workers available to be taxed to fund Social Security benefits is declining, while the quantity of people who have reached age 65 and beyond rises. This structural contradiction can only end in eventual shortfalls. You should plan accordingly. If you are ill-prepared to save, the United States will have a brigades move back in with grandmothers and grandfathers: borrowers are unable to support themselves in retirement.

This chapter reveals why you should start investing money and how best to proceed. Over two-thirds of all American households have savings residing in stocks, bonds, mutual funds, and other accounts. As an African-American, you have access to a golden opportunity - serious growth of your portfolio because the amount of saved money in the stock market lights the way for your family's future. Remember to have at least three months' savings on hand before investing for financial growth.

CHAPTER 17

Seeking Professional Financial Advice

Also, if you have student loans you cannot afford, consult an attorney. There have been people who have gotten out of portions of their student loans by having them re-structured as a result of being declared a hardship case and receiving income-based repayment options. If you have a co-signed loan, that is also something that you might want to let affected parties know about prior to entering into a negotiation. If you think that it may take years to become solvent, seriously consider bankruptcy. This is a very important part of the debt detox and it will be discussed further in Chapter 9. Remember, the people and businesses you owe money to may be able to recoup their losses and reorganize and make a better quality of life for themselves in the long run; you are not the only priority. Conversely, credit card companies and so on are not going anywhere and the government allows for an equitable reorganization for just about everybody.

If you have tried to solve your debt issues on your own, or it is incredibly obvious that you are in over your head, and you are not an expert yourself, go to talk to a professional immediately. There are many competent not-for-profit credit counselors, financial advisors, and debt consolidation and home counseling experts in the market. If you have any collateral tied up in your business, there are people who can help you. All business counseling is done for free and is confidential. Just start at the Better Business Bureau, and that way you will not run up more bills by dealing with predatory companies. There are also a number of national businesses through the American Association of Debt Management Organizations and the Association of Independent Consumer Credit Counseling Agencies who are ethical and certified to help you refine your financial strategy. Just make sure you stay away from people soliciting you on the phone, at home, and at the grocery store.

CHAPTER 18

Protecting Your Financial Health

One contributing editor of a major women's magazine confided to us that she is nearly $100,000 in credit card debt. With this much of the usual 18 percent interest, if she continued to maintain only the total minimum monthly payments, the increasing financial burden would soon be so great that she would have to write a check for over $2,000 each month just to break even. If people don't get their spending under control, combined with the exorbitant interest rates that were scheduled to rise, and it's going to affect everyone - jobs, income, and everything. Economists anticipate that businesses who owe money will be forced to cut back, reduce purchases, and lay off workers. Many people who have helped themselves in the past through cash advances will automatically cut out all non-cash spending when they sense a crack in the financial atmosphere. This fear psychology can impact the economy in a very negative way.

In the past, when things felt really good, you might have treated your finances with as little respect, care, and caution as you have your body. But what use are a flat stomach, shining skin, and a healthy heart if you are financially wrecked and in danger of personal disaster? Few things can make you feel worse than the realization that even though you are now at your most attractive, interesting, and intelligent, you may nonetheless be saddled with overwhelming financial problems.

CHAPTER 19

Teaching Financial Literacy to Others

I realized that my former students really represent a crisis in our communities when I started to work with a West Point student who in her junior year was chosen as the spokesperson of her class. She began to invite me to speak to seniors of her high school and eventually to other local high schools in Brooklyn to help students learn about the financial aid opportunities. I am pleading to all of us to please stand up together and stop each person we know who is about to make a financial, naïve, decision, and to do so continuously, to those closest to us until it becomes socially unacceptable to walk around without basic knowledge of financing a higher education and ignoring all of the financial literacy classes offered everywhere around us.

My next three students were career-changing professionals in their late thirties who were taking my course at UCLA. I also gave a reference for their loan as well. A single mother of two and a nurse was awarded a scholarship to UCLA; she had a lucrative offer to attend a for-profit institution and borrowed every penny she was offered because she "really wanted to go to UCLA." Her story was so common. I always saw students' loans as my responsibility and many times I would have loved to grab the pen and sign all of these loan checks by myself as the last sacred warriors of the old guard that needed to protect the young ones from their financial mistakes.

Maintaining a Healthy Financial Lifestyle

2. Update your financial goals quarterly. During the first few hours of the first day of the new quarter, spend ten minutes updating your nine-month plan, your one- to two-year plan, and your long-term (five-year or more) financial goals. Reflect and see where you are in relation to your financial objectives. Also, where possible, check your taxes. Maybe there are some breaks you can tweak, legally. Do this early in the quarter so any adjustments can take immediate effect. If there are outstanding debts, decide how you will balance paying them off with pursuing these other plans. Sometimes you'll need the flexibility of credibly adjusting your financial resources to meet more pressing needs. Be realistic and flexible with your finances. No outsider knows what's best for you. Keep in mind that goals may change according to life events.

1. Money troubles can happen again. Be vigilant. This doesn't mean stick your head in the sand, sure of impending financial doom. It's simply a caution to remain aware and take charge

of your finances so you don't slip into those bad habits that led you to financial distress previously. Periodically reviewing your banking, credit card, and spending habits is healthy. Make time to sit alone with your monthly budget. Highlight differences between what you planned on spending and where you are actually spending. Pay special attention to the little recurrent expenses that have become a part of your life. For instance, are you consuming more electricity by running a too-hot clothes dryer when there's Californian desert sun waiting to more effectively do the job?

CHAPTER 21

Celebrating Milestones and Successes

Celebrate the milestones. Let me repeat that. Celebrate the milestones. A kid went another day without piano lessons? Celebrate it! Celebrate that you hate your job but went another day without quitting. Remember what Danny DeVito said. "We're not conceited, we're convinced." Are you truly convinced that you can succeed and deserve to succeed? If so, when you do 5 sit-ups, play Rocky's theme. Did you get $100.00 closer to reaching financial freedom? Yip-ee, wow! It was earned, and it's okay to brag a little. Brag a lot. And feel fine about it. Yes, yes, celebrate every moment, every milestone. Celebrate those achievements! Time. To. Brag. Heck, it's not conceited; it's convincing. On the short and long road toward reaching the goal of becoming debt-free, it might be a clichéd phrase and it might sound like an ancient BOA expression, but it couldn't be truer. Just do it. Celebrate the success, the milestones. Celebrate you! You're not finished; you're full-steam-ahead just like a runaway train. And gosh are you chugging along. Celebrate the successes. Celebrate you!

If you're trying to dig yourself out of a financial hole, you know how hard it is. Chances are that former habits that placed you in your financial hole were fun; froth on the top of the cappuccino of life. Now those habits are history and in Sumatra they call you up and whisper, "Why aren't you visiting?" In Tuscany they blare old Beatles tunes and cry, "We can work it out." There are sacrifices. Financial fasts, severe financial diets, are not nearly as much fun as the wind-in-the-face, careless spending that got you into a financial problem. So how do you keep chugging along this long, hard road, putting distance between you and your financial past, when the destination seems so far away?

CHAPTER 22

Overcoming Financial Setbacks

A surprise setback that makes it impossible for you to do what you were planning is something that you are likely to remember for decades afterward. The good news is that the seemingly permanent or insurmountable setbacks that we remember usually don't even come close to meeting the definition. Most setbacks that seem insurmountable when you are living through them are soon forgotten after they have served their purpose (which is to help us learn). As is often said, the setbacks that don't kill us make us stronger, and life is better because we moved on from our setbacks. Generally speaking, people who use the resources in their environment more effectively than others tend to experience more learning and more improvement over time than those who learn and improve more slowly. So the key to life is finding and fitting in to environments where you can learn actively.

No one wants a setback. They are almost universally considered to be unpleasant experiences. Setbacks are a signal that something you were trying to do didn't work out, and you don't get to ignore them. You have to stop what you were doing, look around to find out what went wrong, and adjust your path through life in order to avoid repeating whatever it was that failed. This process is called "learning," and it is the way that successful people get to be successful. When you experience a setback in life, consider that as being given a surprise opportunity to learn and grow - don't let it send you on a shame spiral.

CHAPTER 23

Dealing with Financial Stress

Sometimes, talking to a professional is the first step you need to take to feel better about the situation. Before working with a financial adviser or debt counselor, you should make sure that both you and the counselor see eye to eye on how you got into this financial situation and how you should get out of it. If someone is too sympathetic toward your struggle, then they may not be as focused as they should be on Scripture's many doctrines regarding money and borrowing money. On the other hand, if a professional is an overly strict, inflexible zealot when it comes to debt, they may not be willing to adjust the plan if your situation changes. You need to make sure they understand that the welcome relief of bankruptcy isn't a guaranteed blessing in every situation and that part of your Christian and ethical duty is to settle your debts whenever possible. After all, that's God's advice for you, too!

If you're feeling extremely overwhelmed, either because your finances are in extreme disarray or because you or someone you know has experienced a life-changing experience, it may be beneficial to see a financial adviser, attorney, or other financial planner. Financial stress can cause major insomnia, so you not only need to keep your eyes open for signs of unmanageable stress, but also should be proactive in scheduling financial checkups. There are times when people should absolutely talk to professionals, and many should be speaking with professionals but aren't. One of the greatest feelings I've had is when a reader tells me that the book has finally prompted them to seek professional help in sorting through the many stresses associated with their financial lives. Kudos to them for taking that step!

CHAPTER 24

Balancing Debt Repayment and Enjoyment

After moving to Detroit with her husband in 2007, Hannah Gurman, 37, an assistant professor of history at New York University, experienced what she calls the "infamous budget of the life of a graduate student," which involved stacking processed cheese slices on one's macaroni because they were cheaper than extra-virgin olive oil. In 2012, after Gurman adopted two children from the foster-care system and then had a baby, she and her husband devised a budget to pay down student loans and credit-card debt. That plan included a snowball method and thrifty ideology that made it nearly impossible for them to have any fun at all. In theory, the Gurmans knew that they might be able to pay down their debt faster by scrimping, but they also realized that they could be dead tomorrow. They didn't want to miss their children's younger years. Life was tension-filled.

Shedding debt is not the end goal of your life, it's the means to an end. And most people do better with difficult long-term goals when they receive immediate short-term rewards. "When individuals reduce their current consumption in the name of saving for the future," one study published in the Journal of Retirement in 2014 reads, "they are, in effect, betting that their future selves—along with an assortment of future situations—will have different needs and preferences. This is a risky gamble, as demonstrated by the benchmark Bernstein feedback loop." The study found that individuals who were rewarded in the short term were more likely to save. In a money context, that means by rewarding yourself for saving in the long term, you're more likely to stick to your plan. And considering the high failure rate of long-range financial goals, it's something everyone should consider.

CHAPTER 25

Setting Long-Term Financial Goals

Here are a few items to ask yourself to get the process started: What are the things in life you hope to achieve or experience? What kind of career do you want to have in the future? What are the big-ticket items you want in the future, such as college for your children, a second home, a better vacation? By setting larger financial goals, you can begin to save and prepare for those goals. And by saving and preparing for those larger goals, you can find it easier to keep from frittering your money away. Remember, setting goals for yourself may seem difficult, but by setting objectives you are giving yourself a target. As you make your budget, you can easily see how much money you can put toward these targets and having a budget makes that target a lot easier to meet.

Once your budget is finished, it's time to look into the future and set long-term financial goals. These goals can range from "buying my first home in three years" to "retire at age 55." The purpose of long-term goals is to keep your eyes on the prize, so to speak. By setting these longer-term objectives, you are keeping yourself motivated and focused on the bigger picture. Every small purchase - like a latte at Starbucks when you're on the go or picking up a pizza for dinner on the way home - adds up to large amounts spent and wasted. It's the little things that often keep you from meeting your larger objectives. By focusing on those bigger, long-term goals, you can keep your spending in check because you can easily see how those small dollar amounts add up to become big dollar amounts that derail you from your goal.

CHAPTER 26

Rebuilding Credit Score

This section on rebuilding your credit is important to read and understand, as well as do. If there are errors on your credit report, get those corrected first. To raise your FICO score to 720 or excellent, you need to: establish new credit by responsibly using credit, establish a record of paying the new credit on time, and then keep your promises to pay on time. Follow these three steps. If you follow all three and do so consistently over time, everyone can help to improve and rebuild their FICO score. Here are some options: get another mortgage, reestablish a bank credit card, buy a different car, or lease a car. I recommend buying instead of leasing, especially for those who have a subprime FICO score.

The FICO score is "like" a three-digit number that tells how responsibly you've managed credit in the past, i.e., your credit score; whether you're considered the type of consumer who carefully manages credit, meaning you pay all your cards off each month; how likely you are to pay your bills on time—every time, i.e., your history of payments. Your credit score, or FICO score, will be from 300 to 850. Excellent credit is 720 or greater. Scores falling past 680 are considered good. A FICO score of 650 or 670 is considered fair, and 600 and lower is not good, okay, bad, and embarrassing, correctively.

Once you're without credit cards, you have an excellent chance to rebuild your credit score and reap the rewards of a higher credit score. This is a big plus, not only for your future but also for how much you pay for essentials like car and home insurance, basic utilities, and future loans. With few exceptions, the higher your FICO (credit) score, the less you pay for the same insurance or services that others with lower FICO scores pay. That's right, you can and usually do pay more because of your FICO score. I've had every type of credit situation play out with my clients. Here are a couple of examples:

CHAPTER 27

Exploring Debt Forgiveness Options

If you cannot afford to pay your debts or face losing essential materialistic things (food, clothing, and shelter), bankruptcy might be the right option for you. However, you should thoroughly explore less severe options before considering bankruptcy. If your financial problems are a result of unexpected events such as medical emergency, unemployment, and natural catastrophe, you should definitely consider filing bankruptcy -- especially if you face the risk of losing necessary and important materialistic things. If your financial problems are a result of poor judgement or lack of planning, you should first explore less severe options, stop unnecessary expenses, and implement individual long-term financial plan fully before considering bankruptcy.

Should I consider bankruptcy?

They'll pile up, rob you of your peace of mind, steal your dreams one after another, haunt you in your sleep, keep you in the debt prison! You'll lose access to necessary and important materialistic things that the money could bring: food, clothing, roof over head, transportation, levels of social interactions, health benefits, and most essential resource to perform in the society, time. When you don't have the luxury of time, your "productivity" always declines, and at some point in time, you feel like a complete failure in life. Seems like highly fabricated theory? Not really! If your debts and expenses are out of control and you cannot afford to pay them, contact a reputable credit counselor or reputable attorney.

What happens when I can't pay my bills?

CHAPTER 28

Understanding Bankruptcy

We can opine uncleverly all we choose about how personal values or thoughts or comfort or nourishment might change or disappear with time or awakened circumspection, for opinions and trite hieratic schmaltz about worth and integrity always seem inadequate or inaccurate or dishonest, to me. But we cannot describe the murk and transcendence of losing what was ours, or what we believed was ours; that our possessions had become our spirits, or that everything we owned had defined our beings. To the bankruptcy-troubled at initiation and discharge, whether inappropriately ambitious in failure or not, budget valkries may descend with the promises of destiny and adjustments and overhauls, or other amorphous superstition we dare not dismiss because marvelous bolts of sheer chance.

On June 23, I celebrated the one-year anniversary of my discharge in a Chapter 7 bankruptcy, the kind in which I could eliminate my debt - the most significant minefield between me and a better existence - entirely, with the exceptions of student loans, recent taxes, secured debts, fines, and child support or alimony obligations. The bankruptcy has thus far existed in three stages: filing in November 2008 (the preceding years having fattened up the food chain's buzzards and rendered the operation imperative), sweating the filth of non-dischargeable debt and too much lawyer's fees, living with it for a while after my discharge, and finally, a few months into the life of a World Without Credit, tweaking the chapters and introducing the ever-blackening Greek Chorus of new inquiries.

CHAPTER 29

Navigating Student Loan Debt

Higher education financing comes in many forms, from scholarships, grants, and work-study to federal student loans and private education loans that run the gamut from loans for K-12 education to graduate school financing. Although private loans have no course of study or school type restrictions and offer borrowers several repayment options, they are typically more expensive than federal student loans and federal PLUS loans for parents or graduate students (Grad PLUS loans). PLUS loans require the buyer undergo a credit check and unlike the student loans, Grad PLUS and Parent PLUS are based on credit, interest rates on Direct PLUS loans are set. These limitations are also the case for federal student loans and PLUS loans for graduate students and parents as well as private non-federal student loans for college students.

Let me unpack a few critical key points to decode student loans. First of all, about half of all college students who attend a four-year school graduate with some amount of student loan debt. Private loans can be more expensive and less flexible than federal student loans, which come with standard repayment plans that can cap monthly payments based on income and offer larger interest rate subsidies while you're in school. When possible, try to avoid private student loans because they're typically not eligible for the same sorts of repayment breaks that federal student loans are. Some parents opt to take out federal loans to help their kids go to college, though doing so requires them to apply for a Parent PLUS loan, which requires a credit check. If you think you might want to help your children pay for college, it would be a good idea to make sure that your credit is sound.

CHAPTER 30

Managing Medical Debt

• The large number of sites providing general debt advice notwithstanding, I was unable to locate a dedicated site handling only medical debt. Hence, in this chapter, I grouped suitable resources by two main headings: Non-profit and For-profit. Where there were numerous national organizations, the most appropriate ones were selected and provided with brief descriptions. Because many borrowers need help from local sources, two states (Kentucky and Arizona) are also included. Persons needing help should consider contacting one or more of the organizations listed in this chapter. Many of them provide guidance on how to solve medical debt problems and prepare a realistic budget. Readily available links that can be found online, use search phrases like "help with medical debt" and "get help with medical debt". Some of the national organizations may be applicable to everyone, but most of them could be useful to only a small number, or just a single person when in specific circumstances.

• Whenever the subject of dealing with debts comes up, I hear the same few questions repeated by numerous people. It is to address those frequent questions that I grouped the themes covered in the previous chapters under six main headings: (1) Managing Credit Card Debt. (2) Handling Other Unsecured Debts. (3) Coping with Vehicle Repossession. (4) Handling Home Foreclosure and (5) Managing Medical Debt and (6) Reconstructing Your Financial Life. Prominent among those questions are: What should I do? Where do I start? What action should I take now? Are there any organizations that can help me? In what order should I address my debts? Most of the people seeking help have more than one type of debt. The chapter Managing Credit Card Debt provides the answer for where they should start. There, all the options available for dealing with credit card debts are discussed with special focus on the least stressful, least expensive, and fastest methods that have worked for many people.

CHAPTER 31

Planning for Retirement

If your employer offers matching funds as part of a 401(k) (or similar employer-sponsored retirement plan), that translates to free money in your retirement account – so grab the match by contributing enough to the plan to get the maximum match from your employer. Once you have done that, evaluate whether contributing more to a Roth IRA or into a traditional IRA. Whichever choice you make, you can contribute up to $5,500 (for 2017 or 2018) and if you are age 50 or older, you can make an additional "catch-up" contribution of $1,000. That's a combined $6,500 (for 2017 or 2018) allowed in an IRA plus $18,000 in a 401(k). For workers age 50 and over, there are age-catch up provisions permitted under the tax code – so look into those for each year they are available. If you have money saved up in non-retirement savings, you can also build retirement cash by saving $5 a day. By saving $5 a day in a high-yield savings account or money market fund, you can accumulate roughly $40,000 over the course of a decade.

Start now. There are many reasons to begin planning for your retirement as early as possible. For one, the earlier you start saving, the less money you will have to put away each month to meet your goals. The interest and earnings will build over the years from the time your retirement accounts are established and you will be able to take better advantage of the miracle of compound interest. Second, if retirement planning is part of a long-term financial plan, if investments fall, then you have a longer time frame in which to make up losses, while retirement is still years away. Finally, retirement may be more active than you ever imagined and that takes money.

CHAPTER 32

Conclusion

To go over briefly, the changes that were made with you on your journey were grounded in the connection that you have to the dollars and cents as well as the connection between the you that you are now and the you that you want to be. The practice of meditation, which was incorporated with that which you wish to progress towards, helps you to "see" what you were doing to yourself in a way that caused those "ah ha!" moments that seemed to come during your meditation sessions. Becoming consistent with writing in your journal only reinforced the sense of offense and for some, created an urgency to cleanse itself from the still growing burden of debt. Healthy eating reflects the simplicity that easily helped with the clear thinking that surely helped, especially in the beginning when everything is telling us to take the easy way out, to take the long and harder road to wealth. The application of font not only ushered you to the days of plenty but further broke down frustration by giving you measurable, daily potential in preparation for them.

Congratulations! You have completed the debt detox. With the hard work out of the way, you will be relieved to hear that the rest is relatively easy. This book was only meant to provide a brief education to help you get a renewed, and in many ways, a reborn financial life. Many people have no form of financial education and spiraling out of control with debt is one of the easiest things to do. It is my hope that my words help you live a freer life, one not wed to debt but to possibilities. If you continue being mindful of both your income and spending and regularly consult with your mind and pen, the troubled financial waters that you once sailed will soon be a distant memory and the wealth that you desired at the start of this journey will slowly and surely nourish the seed you planted at those last moments when the journey began.

9 798886 938704